Introduction

2019 celebrates the 100th year of bus operations in Edinburgh. From Edinburgh Corporation Transport, through its renaming as Lothian Region Transport in 1975 and its privatisation as Lothian Buses in 2000, the current company is the largest municipally owned bus company in the UK, retaining its distinguished madder and white livery. The multi-award-winning Lothian family comprises the Lothian City fleet which operates mainly within the Edinburgh and immediate areas, East Coast Buses providing links with East Lothian and Midlothian, Lothian Country serving South Queensferry and parts of West Lothian, Airlink and Skylink linking Edinburgh Airport with the city centre, Ocean Terminal, Fort Kinnaird and Cameron Toll, Lothian Motorcoaches (including an impressive heritage fleet of vintage Edinburgh and former London Routemaster buses), Edinburgh Bus Tours and Night Buses.

The company operates from six depots: Lothian at Annandale Street (Central), Marine and Longstone, East Coast Buses (at Musselburgh and North Berwick) and Lothian Motorcoaches at Newbridge and Lothian Country operates its South Queensferry Service from Central and West Lothian routes from Deans in Livingston.

I grew up in the 1960s and my memories begin with the graceful Leyland Titans – Edinburgh's answer to the London Routemaster. My favourite buses over the years have to be the Alexander-bodied Leyland Atlanteans, of which the Edinburgh Corporation fleet had many. The most interesting periods for me were post-deregulation in the 1980s and the current emergence of the Lothian family of bus and coach services mentioned above.

For this book I have attempted to compile a selection of photos that illustrate recent deliveries of vehicles and the areas that they work in together with some comparison pictures from the past. Some locations may have changed while others remain remarkably the same. This is not intended to be a history of the company and neither tries to cover a full 100 years nor show every type of vehicle operated. Rather, it is a collection of the buses I have grown up with and what I hope are interesting and rare views.

My special thanks go to Keith A. Jenkinson and John Sinclair for encouraging me to produce this book, Gavin Booth and John Allison for inspiring me to take bus photos and for providing some of their excellent photographs, and to Alistair Train, Gordon Scott, Stuart Montgomery, Steve Johnson, Alan Rintoul, Chris Cuthill, Donald Stirling, Bruce McMillan and Dylan Heggie for their photographic contributions and advice.

Lothian's 100-seated Euro 6 Enviro400XLB tri-axle buses were developed in conjunction with ADL and Volvo. Newly built 1101 (SJ19 OXU) is seen leaving ADL's Falkirk factory in February 2019. The number 101 has significance, as will be explained later in the book.

Lothian's previous ADL order was in 2011 for fifteen Eviro 400Hs which were initially diesel-electric hybrids. 213 (SN61 BCE) was painted in the same style of livery to the XLBs in February 2019 with Lothian City fleetnames and Edinburgh Corporation Transport crests. It is seen at the Western Harbour terminus of service 10.

LOTHIAN BUSES 100 YEARS AND BEYOND

RICHARD WALTER

AMBERLEY

Front cover: 1024 (LXZ 5409), one of fifty refurbished former London Metroline Wright-bodied Volvo B9TLs at the University of Edinburgh Kings Buildings terminus of service 41.

Rear cover: Passing the access road to Tantallon Castle in East Lothian is Scania OminCity 20944 (SN57 DCE) on the open-top East Coast Tour.

First published 2019

Amberley Publishing
The Hill, Stroud
Gloucestershire, GL5 4EP

www.amberley-books.com

ISBN 978 1 4456 9189 3 (print)
ISBN 978 1 4456 9190 9 (ebook)

British Library Cataloguing in Publication Data.
A catalogue record for this book is available from the British Library.

Typesetting by Aura Technology and Software Services, India. Printed in the UK.

Former London Metroline Wright-bodied Volvo Gemini B9TL 1006 (LXZ 5388) heads back to the Kings Road terminus at Marine Garage after a morning rush journey on service 19. The purchase of these second-hand buses helped accelerate the process of the Lothian fleet becoming fully Euro V or Euro VI compliant.

A fresh repaint for Alexander-bodied Leyland Atlantean 364 (SSF 364H) at Seafield works prior to wheelnut guard-rings being replaced. These little presentational touches made the Lothian fleet stand out from other operators. The Lothian Regional Council crests replaced the original Edinburgh Corporation Transport crests in 1975. (John Allison)

Lothian Motorcoaches has inherited a number of fine preserved Edinburgh vehicles, which are available for private hire and weddings. They also appear on annual running days along key Edinburgh routes. Seen in September 2017 are 1949 Metro-Cammell-bodied Daimler CVG6 135 (FSC 182) and 1988 Alexander RH Leyland Olympian 322 (E322 MSG).

Classic Bus Running Days have always been popular. This photograph shows a fine line-up of vintage Edinburgh buses in St Andrew Square, headed up by 1972 Alexander AL Leyland Atlantean AN68/1R 1 (BSF 1L) – initially preserved by the Lothian Bus Club and affectionately known as *Basil* due to its registration.

Approaching Fairmilehead terminus on a Classic Bus Running Day is preserved 1954 Metro-Cammell Weymann Orion Leyland Titan PD2/20 480 (LFS 480).

1954 Metro-Cammell Weymann Orion Leyland Titan PD2/20 433 (LFS 433) is seen on the 21 to Greendykes in the company of a number of Leyland Atlanteans on the Bridges – a view that has barely changed in recent times. (Gavin Booth Collection)

1964 Alexander E-bodied Leyland Titan PD3/6 673 (ASC 673B) was one of a number of similar vehicles to carry broadside advertising – in this case for Cutty Sark Blended Scotch Whisky. Note the tram board it carries for Edinburgh Zoo, which service 26 still serves – albeit now with Volvo Geminis carrying special branding.

1964 Alexander E-bodied Leyland Titan PD3/6 675 (ASC 675B) followed by 1962 Alexander Leyland Titan PD2A/30 611 (YWS 611), both on service 12, are seen crossing the Mound while heading towards the West End. 611 is now fully preserved. (Gavin Booth Collection)

The fleet number 101 will always be special in the history of Edinburgh buses. The latest vehicle to carry the number is 2004 Wright Eclipse-bodied Volvo B7RLE TB101 (SN04 NFZ) – one of eight with the driver training school. It is seen leaving Queen Margaret University in Musselburgh while on training duties.

An earlier shot of 2004 Wright Eclipse-bodied Volvo B7RLE 101 (SN04 NFZ) while still in public service with branding for Night Buses. It is pictured leaving the old approach road to the Royal Infirmary of Edinburgh on service 18. In 2018 route 18 was renumbered 400, operated by Skylink deckers and extended from the Gyle Centre to Edinburgh Airport.

Nearing the end of its long service is the unique 1961 Alexander Y Type-bodied Leyland Leopard PSU3/2R 101 (YSG 101). The photo was taken at the former Oxgangs terminus, where it had just completed a part route service 16 before returning to Central Garage.

1961 Alexander Y Type-bodied Leyland Leopard PSU3/2R 101 (YSG 101) was delivered as an experimental three-door vehicle with conductor with passengers boarding by the rear door. It was later converted to single-door and painted in black and white coach livery and used on the airport service. Its last years on the road saw it back in madder and white livery and one-man operated. It also spent a while as a non-mobile training vehicle at Marine. On withdrawal it was sold for preservation and is seen at an event at St Giles.

This scenic view of former London Metroline Wright-bodied Volvo B9TL 1025 (LXZ 5411) was taken at Silverknowes, which used to be served by a number of routes. Unused for some years, during 2017 route 29 from Gorebridge was extended to the promenade.

Alexander-bodied Leyland Atlantean 268 (WFS 268K) approaches Elm Row – the traditional change-over point for drivers from Central Garage for services travelling to and from Leith. (John Allison)

The steep climb to Clermiston featuring 2017 Wright StreetAir electric bus 289 (SK67 FLH) on route 1, which used to complete a full circle but now operates only from Easter Road to Clermiston.

1966 Alexander A-bodied Leyland Atlantean PDR1/1 802 (EWS 802D) was one of two of the first batch of single-door rear-engined vehicles to feature panoramic windows, which later deliveries would have as standard. The 86 (and 85) were limited stop services running initially from Eastfield to Clermiston. The routes are now covered by high-frequency services 26 and X26, which serve Tranent and Seton Sands in East Lothian.

An overhead view of 2017 Wright StreetAir electric bus 285 (SK67 FLD) on Waterloo Place. The buses have charging station facilities at Central Garage and can be fully charged in three to four hours and can operate for up to 130 miles on electric power. The buses carry the fleetname Lothian Electric.

2017 Wright StreetAir electric bus 286 (SK67 FLE) is one of six similar buses for use primarily on services 1, 24, 60 and 61. Occasionally they appear on other routes such as the 45 and 286 is seen on the approach to Queen Margaret University in Musselburgh.

In 2014 Lothian Buses trialled demonstrator Wright Gemini 3-bodied Volvo B5TL BF63 HDC, which was given fleet number 286. It was used mainly on service 27 and was photographed leaving Hunters Tryst en route to Silverknowes. Copyright issues over the style of glazed staircases on the Wright-bodied New Routemasters for London meant that this demonstrator featured a rather unattractive layout which was vastly improved for subsequent Lothian orders.

Another demonstrator was evaluated in 2017. Wright Streetlite Micro Hybrid SK17 HHL appeared on routes 1, 6, 24 and 36.

Back in 1989, Lothian Region Transport (LRT) explored the options of alternative fuel when they borrowed Northern Counties Prestidge-bodied DAF SB220 – a gas bus demonstrator. It is seen on the 13 route at Charlotte Square. Route 13 is currently operated by Edinburgh Coach Lines.

Service 49 has seen a variety of single and double-deck buses over the years. WX08 WFN was a Wright Eclipse-bodied MAN which Lothian Buses trialled against its Volvo machines. In this picture the bus is passing under the rail bridge at Cameron Toll on to Old Dalkeith Road.

Prior to ordering Scania OmniCities for Airlink duties, during 2004 Lothian Buses acquired demonstrator East Lancs-bodied OmniDekka SNO4 CPE, numbering it 999 and decking it out in full harlequin livery. The bus was principally used on the busy cross-city service 37 and is seen near Cameron Toll while heading for Penicuik in Midlothian.

Lothian Buses has trialled a couple of bendy buses, one of which was 2004 Scania CN94UA YN54 ALO, numbered 50 and complete in Park & Ride livery as worn by the Dennis Darts and Plaxton Tridents used on limited stop service X48 between Ingliston and Sheriffhall Park & Ride facilities. The photo was taken at the press launch at Sheriffhall.

An oddity in the current fleet is Caetano-UVG Urbanstar-bodied Dennis Dart SLF A01 (V664 FPO), formerly with Doig's of Glasgow. It has been used as a mobile ticket office and for other company publicity. Since acquired, it has appeared in a number of different liveries and promoted Transport for Edinburgh as well as Lothian Buses. It is seen heading up Annandale Street in its latest style.

Prior to East Coast Buses taking over the running of two Midlothian services from Lothian Buses, and service 39 being shortened from Gorebridge to the Midlothian Community Hospital in Dalkeith and renumbered as the 139, this Mercedes-Benz Citaro K demonstrator, BN17 JVC, was used in service during September 2017. In this view it is approaching Dalkeith from Woodburn.

Coaching is not new in Lothian. For many years the black and white-liveried single-deck coaches and double-deck buses were a familiar sight on airport services, limited stop rushes and private hires. One-off Caetano Optimo 70 (L70 LRT) is seen with more traditional coaches at Murrayfield while awaiting passengers from a rugby game.

Prior to the disappearance of coaches for a number of years, the coaching fleet lost its black and white livery in favour of madder and white. Contrasting with the previous photo, here is Caetano Optimo 70 (L70 LRT) showing the revised colours.

A couple of new Alexander Dennis Enviro400XLB-bodied Volvo B8L tri-axle buses seen on delivery to Edinburgh in December 2018. (Gordon Scott)

The previous ADL order was back in 2011 when the Scottish Government's Green Bus funding allowed the purchase of fifteen Alexander Dennis integral Enviro 400H diesel-electric hybrid buses. This impressive view shows a number of buses on their delivery to Edinburgh in a new variation of the madder livery based on Winter Gold and Radiance Red. (Steve Johnson)

Another shot of the then state-of-the-art buses on delivery from Falkirk. A few of the buses received special themed registrations, as can be seen in this photograph. (Steve Johnson)

Arriving at Seafield, and nearly at Lothian Buses' Seafield works, the new hybrid fleet displays a variety of short side slogans to encourage car drivers to change their behaviour to a more sustainable transport mode.

Following the success of the Edinburgh Classic Tour set up in 1989, LRT expanded operations over the border. Seen headed up by open-top converted Alexander-bodied Leyland Atlantean 49 (BFS 49L), a convoy of buses is about to leave Waverley Bridge for its new home in Oxford, where a tour was introduced in conjunction with local operator Tappins.

Another Classic Tour was introduced in Cambridge with a later batch of Leyland Atlanteans. The photo shows the convoy on its way to its new operating area. (Alan Rintoul)

In December 2016, Service 22 was given a big boost by the introduction of twenty-five Euro 6 Wrightbus Gemini 3-bodied Volvo B5TLs. On 13 December a parade of some of the new vehicles took place along Princes Street.

Following the procession through the city centre, two of the new Wrightbus Gemini 3-bodied Volvo B5TLs were displayed to the public by the Usher Hall on Lothian Road. Even Santa Claus came along to have a look!

A second batch of twenty-five Wrightbus Gemini 3-bodied Volvo B5TLs arrived in the summer of 2017. Seen at the launch at Edinburgh Zoo, these buses were allocated to Marine depot for use on service 26 between Clerwood and Tranent or Seton Sands. During 2018 all the buses picked up zoo branding with various animals and birds featured on the sides and rears. (Gordon Scott)

In 1999, Lothian Buses took delivery of its first low-floor buses, which were also the first to feature a new harlequin livery. Alexander ALX400-bodied Dennis Tridents 501–505 (T501–505 SSG) were pictured at the official launch at Ocean Terminal. Further deliveries would feature Plaxton President bodywork. All of these buses were later converted to open-top for the City Sightseeing fleet.

Edinburgh Bus Tours operates under the identities of City Sightseeing, Edinburgh Tours and Majestic Tours. A fleet of brand-new Wright Eclipse Gemini 3-bodied Volvo B5TLs was delivered in 2016 and a launch was held in the Grassmarket. Being piped there down Johnston Terrace are a trio of the buses in the three tour liveries.

Wright Eclipse Gemini 3-bodied Volvo B5LHs 243 (SJ16 ZZG), 221 (SJ16 SCF) and 234 (SJ16 CTX) pose for photos at the Grassmarket launch of the new tour vehicles.

Secured through additional Scottish Green Bus funding, Lothian Buses took delivery of the first ten of fifty Volvo 7900H hybrid buses in 2013. Piped onto Castle Street by Gordon Stirling for a public launch is bus 1 (LB13 BUS), seen displaying a green ribbon on the front for the cutting ceremony.

Volvo 7900H hybrid buses 2 (HY13 BUS), 1 (LB13 BUS) and 3 (SN13 BCY) being inspected by passers-by on Castle Street under the iconic Edinburgh Castle.

During 2018, Thorntons Bus Refurbishment of Ashington upgraded ten of Lothian's Wrightbus Gemini-bodied Volvo B9TLs to very high coach standards for the Lothian Motorcoaches fleet. Four of the buses, including 848 (re-registered to MXZ 1758), are seen in convoy on Princes Street following a private hire.

Also given a public launch on Castle Street in 2011 were Alexander Dennis Enviro400H diesel-electric hybrid buses 215 (SN61 BCK), 207 (SN61 BBK), 206 (SN61 BBJ) and 202 (HY61 BUS).

The company took delivery of 192 Plaxton President-bodied Dennis Tridents between June 1999 and June 2004. A handful remain in service at the time of writing this book. Representing the last batch bought are 696 (SN04 AEL) and 697 (SN04 AEM), pictured at the official launch of the branded service 26 at Our Dynamic Earth by Holyrood.

Lothian Buses held regular bus user events at different locations. 2007 Wrightbus Eclipse Urban-bodied Volvo B7RLE 141 (SK07 CFO) and 2006 Wrightbus Gemini-bodied Volvo B9TL 803 (SN56 AFJ) were photographed at Ocean Terminal in branded liveries for services 29 and 37.

A bright sunny morning on Edinburgh Castle Esplanade in 1991 saw the launch of LRT's only batch of Leyland Lynx buses. 186 (H186 OSG) is seen heading the display. These were the only dual-door examples in the UK.

It is not quite such a sunny morning in the same location twenty-seven years on in December 2018 when the launch of Lothian's Alexander Dennis Enviro400XLB-bodied Volvo B8L tri-axle buses – the first buses in almost twenty years to feature dual doors – took place. 1071 (SG68 LCN), 1070 (SG68 LCM) and 1068 (SG68 LCK) were among the six vehicles at the launch. The buses were re-registered with 19 plates before entering service.

The advertising shown on Alexander Dennis Enviro400XLB-bodied Volvo B8L 1071 (SG68 LCM) mentions the collaboration of Lothian, Alexander Dennis and Volvo. The bus (seen coming down the Mound) was re-registered with 19 plates before entering service.

A very similar side ad appeared on 1992 Alexander R-bodied Leyland Olympian 873 (K873 CSF), seen leaving the Gyle Centre – by which time Volvo had bought Leyland.

L456 JCK was a stepless, easy access bus and another joint venture between Alexanders and Volvo. It was a Swedish manufacturer Säffle-bodied Volvo B10L produced under licence by Alexanders. LRT had the bus on loan in June 1995 and painted it in full livery with fleet number 156 (although it carried fleet number 189 before entering service). It was pictured awaiting Volvo delegates at Edinburgh Airport.

Prior to entry into service on routes 11 and 16 in March 2019, Alexander Dennis Enviro400XLB-bodied Volvo B8L 1063 (SG68 LCA) was used for route trialling and driver familiarisation. It is the only one of the batch to carry a 68 plate.

The Queensferry Crossing Experience in 2017 gave people the opportunity to walk over the new Forth Bridge before it formally opened to traffic. Lothian Buses provided shuttle services and required the use of mainly Wrightbus Gemini 3-bodied Volvo B5TLs, including brand-new vehicles destined for Skylink duties. The picture shows older 434 (SA15 VTN) repainted into Skylink livery, having been new to Airlink in 2015. (Gordon Scott)

This view shows the impressive new bridge and gives an idea of the number of buses that were required for the occasion. (Bruce McMillan)

Wrightbus Gemini 3-bodied Volvo B5TL 470 (SF17 VNE) was borrowed from Marine Garage for shuttle duties at Queensferry. (Bruce McMillan)

For the Commonwealth Games held in Edinburgh during 1986, a similar large number of buses was required to shuttle competitors, staff and spectators. 1982 Alexander RH-bodied Leyland Olympian ONTL11/1R 667 (GSC 667X) was seen awaiting passengers at Meadowbank Stadium.

1983 ECW-bodied Leyland Olympian ONTZ11/2R 706 (A706 YFS) wore a special livery for the 1986 Commonwealth Games and *Daily Record*, and is seen on shuttle bus duties through Holyrood Park.

Seen in the same location and also providing shuttle services for Edinburgh events as part of the 2014 Glasgow Commonwealth Games is brand-new Volvo 7900H 23 (BT14 DKC), which had yet to be used in public service.

For the Edinburgh Moonwalk 2013, Lothian Buses provided special service 50. Alexander Dennis integral Enviro 400H 211 (SN61 BBX) navigates the roundabout at the foot of Easter Road.

Putting some welly into it! A sponsored bus push for charity at Gyle Broadway. 1988 Alexander RH-bodied Leyland Olympian 325 (E325 MSG) was one of the two buses used.

Covered in balloons, single-door 1996 Volvo Royale-bodied Olympian 433 (P433 KSX) is seen being decorated by Bank of Scotland staff for the annual Edinburgh Festival Parade. Delivered in black and white livery, 433 carried several different liveries until its withdrawal in 2011.

More balloons, this time for the Edinburgh Gay Pride parade in 2018, carried by Plaxton President-bodied Dennis Trident 2 217 (XIL 1480) – previously 516 (V516 ESC) in the Lothian Buses and later Edinburgh Bus Tours fleets.

ScotRail has borrowed various buses and coaches for rail replacement services over the years. 1989 Alexander-bodied Leyland Olympian 368 (E368 WSC) awaits passengers at Wallyford station. It was originally delivered in black and white livery for airport services.

In its first year of operation in 2018, Lothian Motorcoaches provided rail replacement services throughout Scotland. Seen at Falkirk Grahamston station is Van Hool 'Acron'-bodied Volvo B12B(T) 9007 (WLT 752), one of four second-hand purchases.

Another view of Plaxton President-bodied Dennis Trident 2 217 (XIL 1480), seen on loan to Lothian Motorcoaches for the Musselburgh Parade in the summer of 2018.

Lothian LRT bought ninety-one Plaxton Pointer Dennis Dart SLFs between 1999 and 2003. Representing the first batch (and first low-floor single-decks for the company) is 169 (V169 EFS), seen on the first day of operation (and official launch) of the 22, serving the Scottish Executive offices at Victoria Quay. Once the nearby Ocean Terminal shopping centre opened, route 22 terminated there instead.

Over the years the annual Royal Highland Show at Ingliston has been well served by Lothian Buses. Over three days in the height of summer it attracts thousands of visitors. ECW-bodied Leyland Olympian ONTZ11/2R 724 (A724 YFS) unloads passengers at the showground.

The Royal Highland Show service running between the showground and Edinburgh city centre was numbered 98. An additional service 97 commenced in 2017, connecting with Edinburgh Gateway and Edinburgh Park train and tram stations. Wrightbus Gemini 3-bodied Volvo B5TL 482 (SF17 VNT) was new and not yet in service when in use on the 98 in 2017.

Following deregulation, the LRT Lothian network was extended into East Lothian, Midlothian and West Lothian. ECW Leyland Olympian 784 (C784 SFS) was from a reduced order of twenty-five buses received in 1985 and was caught in Dalkeith publicising the forthcoming new services.

Twenty-five of the former Metroline refurbished Wright Gemini-bodied Volvo B9TLs were painted into Lothian County livery for expansion into West Lothian during 2018. 1028 (LXZ 5413) was in Bathgate to promote the new routes when this photograph was taken.

While work was underway constructing the Western Approach Road, LRT provided a free bus service linking Morrison Street car park and the West End. Alexander-bodied Leyland Atlantean AN68/1R 609 (OSC 609V) was one of a number of buses used.

The unusual sight of 1982 Leyland National 2 NL116TL11/2R (KSX 105X) exiting Waverley station in the days before all traffic, including taxis, was banned.

A very long way from home! Alexander-bodied 1982 Leyland Atlantean AN68/1R 662 (GSC 662X) disembarking off the Skye ferry in Portree in the days before the bridge was built. The bus (affectionately known as *Anneka*) was on hire to the Lothian Bus Club.

The advert could not have been more appropriate on 1984 ECW Leyland Olympian 745 (B745 GSC), photographed on the top of the Cairngorms on another Lothian Bus Club adventure.

1996 Volvo Royale-bodied Olympian 433 (P433 KSX) in another guise on route 50 serving the original berth of the *Britannia* at Ocean Terminal.

Following a spell as service bus, 1988 Alexander-bodied Leyland Olympian 310 (E310 MSG) transferred to the then LRT tours fleet and was converted to single-door layout – although it remained closed top for a short time. It was pictured carrying out rail replacement duties at Newcraighall station.

Alexander Dennis Enviro400XLB-bodied Volvo B8L 1068 (SG68 LCK) on the cobbles of the famous Royal Mile passing from Castlehill to Lawnmarket with the fascinating Camera Obscura visitor centre in the background. The bus received a 19 plate registration before hitting the road in service.

Nearby at Greyfriars and the famous statue of Greyfriars Bobby (although obscured by the bus) is 1975 Alexander AY-bodied Leyland Leopard PSU3C/4R 125 (MSF 125P) on service 24 – a route that has changed many times over the years.

Lothian Country was originally set up to provide a service from Edinburgh to South Queensferry. 2009 Wrightbus Gemini 2-bodied Volvo B9TL 929 (SN09 CVP), seen with the Forth Rail Bridge in the background, is one of eleven repainted from Lothian Buses livery that operate the 43 and X43.

The same location in the days when LRT service 66 served South Queensferry. Alexander-bodied Leyland Atlantean AN68/1R 616 (OSC 616V) climbs up the hill on its journey back to Edinburgh.

Single-door and coach-liveried Alexander-bodied Leyland Atlantean AN68/1R 664 (GSC 664X), named *Robert Burns*, is also on long service 66 which crossed Edinburgh into East Lothian and terminated at Seton Sands.

Lothian Motorcoaches refurbished Wrightbus Gemini-bodied Volvo B9TL 842 (MXZ 1752), seen here at South Queensferry shadowed by the Forth Road Bridge.

In 2017, Edinburgh Bus Tours introduced a Three Bridges Tour allowing people to travel from Edinburgh to South Queensferry, where they could take a boat tour if they wished. Plaxton President-bodied Dennis Tridents 650 and 651 were painted in special livery for the service and 650 (XIL 1484) is seen with the new Queensferry Crossing in the background.

With the growing popularity of cruise ships coming into the Forth, Lothian introduced express service X99 in 2018 which ran on the days the cruise liners were due into South Queensferry. Wrightbus Gemini 3-bodied Volvo B5TL 1052 (SJ18 NFC) was caught on its return journey into Edinburgh. (Donald Stirling)

Also on Cruiselink X99 duties is similar Wrightbus Gemini 3-bodied Volvo B5TL 1054 (SJ18 NFE), seen loading visitors who are transported from the liners to the shore on small motor launches.

Demonstrating the versatility of duties that they can perform, Lothian Motorcoaches provided buses for linking the car parks in Gullane in East Lothian during the golf championships in 2018. Wrightbus Gemini-bodied Volvo B9TL 842 (MXZ 1752) was one of the vehicles used.

During 2018 and 2019, the hybrid Volvo 7900Hs have been refurbished and repainted in the current fleet livery. 31 (BG64 FXD) passes through Clayknowes on its way into Musselburgh on route 30.

Same location but at a time when a number of second-hand Leyland Nationals had been acquired for a short period. One of these, 127 (FRA 527V), is seen on route 45.

1991 Alexander Dash-bodied Dennis Dart 123 (K123 CSG) passed from the main fleet to MacTours. It is seen heading for Stoneybank on a temporary shuttle bus service.

1984 ECW Leyland Olympian 753 (B753 GSC) was transferred to the MacTours fleet in 2002 for principal use on a free transfer to the Edinburgh Crystal Factory in Penicuik. It was pictured at Stoneybank operating a rail replacement service.

2018 saw the biggest intake of second-hand vehicles for several decades. Fifty former London Wrightbus Gemini-bodied Euro V Volvo B9TLs fitted with emission abatement systems to bring them up to Euro VI compatible standards were sourced through dealer Ensignbus and extensively refurbished before entering service. One of the first two to enter service was former Tower Transit 1002 (LKZ 5384), seen at Granton.

The other side of Granton – no longer served by buses. 1982 Alexander-bodied Leyland Atlantean AN68/1R 630 (CSG 630X) climbs from Granton Square on service 9, which used to operate to Torphin.

Airlink Wrightbus Gemini 3-bodied Volvo B5TL 501 (SF17 VOV), seen leaving Edinburgh Airport. The popular and high-frequency service 100 complements the alternative Edinburgh Trams route. Both have different ways into the city and are well used.

Before Airlink there was Airline. 1989 Alexander-bodied Leyland Olympian ONCL10/2RZ 366 (F366 WSC) was new in black and white coach livery but was repainted in this style in 1995. For a while the 100 terminated at the old St Andrew Square bus station, where 366 is seen picking up passengers. The bus was downgraded to madder and white bus duties in 2000 and painted a lighter red and white for service 15 in 2005.

The earliest deckers used on airport services were from a 1967 delivery of Alexander A-bodied Leyland Atlantean PDR1/1s, which were refurbished and painted black and white. Now preserved in its later livery is 869 (JSC 869E), pictured at Silverknowes on a Classic Bus Running Day.

The first double-deck coaches were replaced in 1982 by five single-door Alexander-bodied Leyland Atlantean AN68/1Rs which were all given the names of famous Scottish authors. 660 (GSC 660X) was *Sir Arthur Conan Doyle* and is seen at Haymarket, heading to Edinburgh Airport.

Leyland Olympians were replaced on Airlink duties by 2000 with Plaxton President-bodied Dennis Trident 2s such as 549 (W549 RSG), pictured leaving Edinburgh Airport.

In the summer of 2006 the first five of fifteen Scania OmniCity buses arrived for Airlink duties. The last of these five took the fleetnumber of the previous OmniDekka demonstrator 999 and was registered SK06 AHN. The vehicle was photographed at Ocean Terminal at a display of disabled access buses. The batch ended their service lives in madder and white on route 35.

Probably the shortest lived buses on the 100 were the 2015 Wrightbus Gemini 3-bodied Volvo B5TLs 426–437, which were replaced in 2017, although 427 remained in Airlink colours until 2018. 432 (SA15 VTL) is seen one foggy evening on Waverley Bridge. 426–430 are now in madder and white and 431–437 are in Skylink blue and white.

Initially Skylink service 200 was operated by single-deck Wrightbus Eclipse 2 Urban Volvo B7RLEs such as 189 (SN13 BFP), seen arriving at Ocean Terminal. The service now requires double-deckers.

During 2018 the route of Skylink service 300 was changed to operate to Cameron Toll rather than Ocean Terminal. Wrightbus Gemini 3-bodied hybrid Volvo B5TL 578 (SJ67 MFV) turns the roundabout at the far end of the Cameron Toll Shopping Centre. A new Skylink service 400 commenced operating to Fort Kinnaird.

Wrightbus Gemini 3-bodied Volvo B5TL 436 (SA15 VTP) is one of the Skylink deckers now operating on service 200 between Edinburgh Airport and Ocean Terminal. It was originally delivered in Airlink livery.

Wrightbus Gemini 2-bodied Volvo B9TL 940 (SN10 DKK) in another Airlink livery prepares to leave a snowy Waverley Bridge in the memorable winter of 2010. The bus is now numbered 20940 in the East Coast Buses fleet.

Edinburgh has suffered some very wintry weather over the years, although in more recent years conditions have been kinder. Alexander-bodied Leyland Atlantean AN68/1R 609 (OSC 609V) is spotted here on a very snowy Frogston Road with a friendly wave from the driver.

This dramatic shot of 1985 ECW-bodied Leyland Olympian 785 (C785 SFS) churning up the snow was taken at Oxgangs.

The heavy snows in 2010 caused much disruption in Edinburgh. Wrightbus Gemini-bodied Volvo B9TL 894 (SN08 BXG) was stuck in snow on the Mound, as was the bus behind.

Unable to move in the snow coming down the Mound on the same day is Plaxton Pointer-bodied Dennis Dart SLF 185 (Y185 CFS).

Snowy but slightly brighter weather for Wrightbus Gemini-bodied Volvo B7TL 744 (SN55 BOJ) as it approaches Queen Margaret University.

Frasers (with its famous musical clock) closed its doors during 2018. Wrightbus Gemini 3-bodied Volvo B5TL 468 (SF17 VHC) passes the store while it was still trading. (Stuart Montgomery)

1984 ECW-bodied Leyland Olympian 768 (B768 GSC) in Bus & Coach Council livery is diverted past Frasers due to road closure on Princes Street.

Route 10 has seen some interesting vehicles over the years. Here, Alexander Dennis Enviro400H 210 (SN61 BBV) nears the Torphin terminus – one of fifteen Hybrid buses allocated from Central Garage in 2011. Following battery issues, many of the batch were retrofitted with diesel engines.

The ill-fated Lothian Region Transport 1982 Alexander RH-bodied Leyland Olympian ONTL11/1R 666 (GSC 666X) – one of a pair which principally ran on services 10 and 24. In this early photo at Torphin terminus, 666 had a Transign front screen which was later replaced with Vultron Metro II dot-matrix screens. In 1987 the bus was destroyed in an arson attack and was broken up for spares.

Leaving the Gyle Centre on service 20 to Ratho is 2007 Wrightbus Eclipse Urban Volvo B7RLE 151 (SN57 DCF).

Wrightbus Gemini 3-bodied Volvo B5TL 1061 (SJ18 NFN), dwarfed by Granton Parish Church on Boswall Parkway.

The arrival of two giant pandas at Edinburgh Zoo prompted this contravision advertising on 2008 Wrightbus Gemini-bodied Volvo B9TL 900 (SN08 BXO), photographed at the zoo entrance.

There have been a number of routes featuring different styles of route branding over the years. 2006 Wrightbus Gemini-bodied Volvo B9TL 767 (SN56 ABZ) was one of several allocated to service 31with the Ace of Spades tag line and is seen heading through Newington.

In black and white coach livery, 1967 Alexander A-bodied Leyland Atlantean PDR1/1 874 (JSC 874E) is seen on service 9 at the east end of Princes Street. Woolworths has long since gone and the bus shelters and stops replaced, but not much else has changed. (John Allison)

Currently being restored for preservation is Alexander J-bodied Leyland Atlantean 300 (WFS 300K), seen here leaving Eastfield terminus on service 49. (John Allison)

Pictured prior to entering service is 294, one of seven Plaxton President Volvo B7TLs. The bus was registered W294 PFS, but due to a paperwork error the registration had also been allotted to a West Midlands bus. 294 was therefore re-registered in late 2000 as W122 DOP until the error was corrected and the original plate could be refitted.

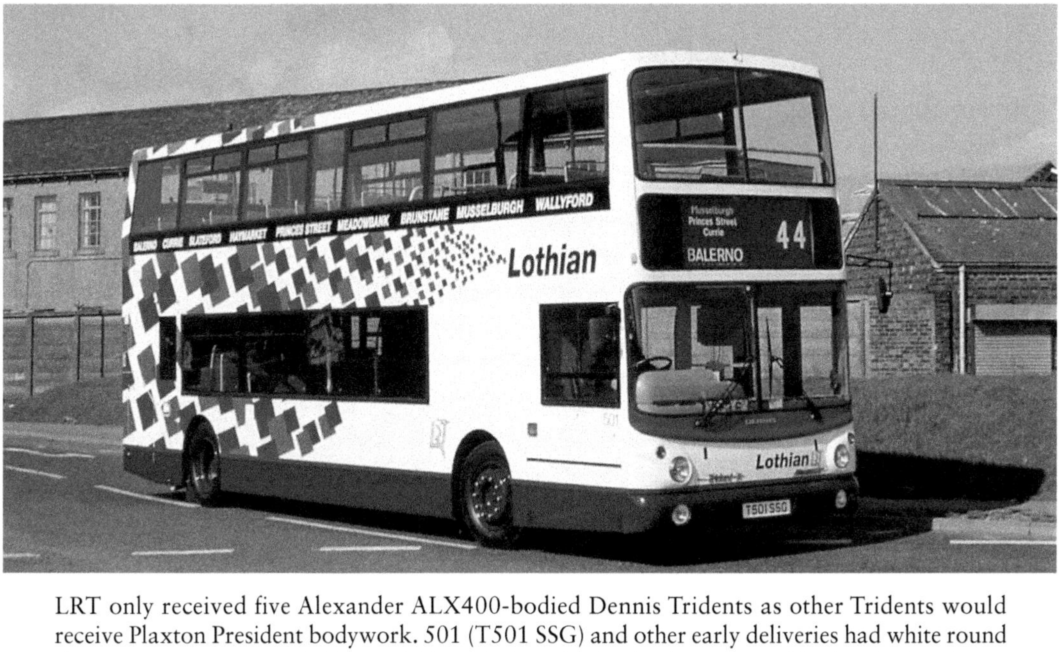

LRT only received five Alexander ALX400-bodied Dennis Tridents as other Tridents would receive Plaxton President bodywork. 501 (T501 SSG) and other early deliveries had white round the destination screens which would have light red added subsequently. The bus had white on black route branding for service 44. A later delivery had white on red branding in a similar style for service 26.

2018 saw a number of all-white buses appearing within the Lothian family. One of the earliest examples of a white bus was 1984 ECW Leyland Olympian 762 (B762 GSC), which ran as such in between all-over advertising campaigns during the 1986 Commonwealth Games when as many buses as possible were required on the road.

Following a spell in poppy vinyls for Remembrance Day 2017, Wrightbus Gemini 3-bodied Volvo B5LH 551 (SN15 VUB) remained in all-white livery, having this company Christmas video advertising applied before remaining in all-over white until the 2018 Poppy campaign. The generic livery allowed the bus to be loaned for spells to East Coast Buses and Lothian Country.

Lothian Country required buses when it commenced its West Lothian operations in 2018 and received four Wright Eclipse 2 Volvo B5LHs from Bullocks of Manchester. 592 (LP11 YAY) rests outside the Livingston Centre. All four buses are white.

Four Skylink Wrightbus Gemini 3-bodied Volvo B5TLs were also painted white in 2018 and have been used for both Lothian Country and Lothian Buses services. 573 (SJ67 MFK) crosses the Royal Mile and High Street onto George IV Bridge on cross-city service 23.

Lothian Buses experimented for a while with an Edinburgh shuttle service. What was offered was not a traditional bus service or a taxi facility. Ford Transit minibuses ran on set routes but could be pre-booked and passengers dropped off at other destinations within a certain radius on request. S2 (SH56 RFF) heads towards Haymarket. (Steve Johnson)

Minibuses returned to the fleet in 2018 when Lothian Motorcoaches added two to its fleet. 9101 (LC68 LMC) is one of a pair of Mercedes-Benz Sprinter 514 CDIs. They feature very high specification interiors, which allow them to be used on both private hire and coach tours.

An example of the smaller bus of the past is 1981 Midibus Duple Dominant-bodied Leyland Cub CU435 170 (HSC 170X), seen in use here as a connecting service on route 16 between Oxgangs and Redford Road during roadworks when larger buses were unable to use the roads.

On diversion at the Tron is Alexander J-bodied Leyland Atlantean 307 (PSC 307G). Note the replacement lower front panel, which is of the type fitted to later deliveries of Atlanteans. (John Allison)

Pictured on the Shore at Leith heading to Ocean Terminal on busy service 22 is Wrightbus Gemini 3-bodied Volvo B5TL 448 (SJ66 LPF).

On diversion by the Water of Leith Walkway is Wrightbus Eclipse Urban Volvo B7RLE 170 (SN58 BYX).

Another example of route branding is seen on Wrightbus Gemini 2-bodied Volvo B9TL 957 (SN11 EAJ), one of twelve vehicles which featured the popular book character Maisie of Morningside created by the late Aileen Paterson. Although intended for use on service 5, buses occasionally strayed on to other routes, as did 957, which is seen on service 44. (Steve Johnson)

Also off its normal service 26 and pictured as it pulls into Wallyford Terminus on the 44 is Edinburgh Zoo-branded Wrightbus Gemini 3-bodied Volvo B5TL 491 (SF17 VOC). Each animal or bird design is displayed on two buses and the whole batch of Marine-based vehicles carry them.

Wrightbus Gemini 2-bodied Volvo B9TL316 (SN09 CUV) wears another Edinburgh Zoo livery. It is seen again not on its usual service 26 but working an evening rush back to Marine Garage on service 15.

As a teaser for the brand-new buses appearing on route 22, two Wrightbus Gemini 2-bodied Volvo B9TLs were debranded and given vinyl red ribbons. 344 (SN59 BGX) is seen at the Gyle.

Lothian Buses has supported Poppy Scotland in recent years by preparing buses in special liveries. Wrightbus Gemini 3 Volvo B5TL 551 (SA15 VUB) is seen at Gyle Broadway featuring the 2017 design.

Carrying the 2018 Poppy Scotland design, Wrightbus Gemini 3 Volvo B5TL 551 (SA15 VUB) is seen arriving at St Andrew Square as part of the commemorative services.

Prior to deciding on the current livery design, a number of single and double-deckers were painted in a more traditional style. Wrightbus Eclipse Urban Volvo B7RLE 162 (SN58 BYO) passes by Kings Buildings at Blackford.

Standing out in bright yellow advertising the 2018 Edinburgh International Festival is Wrightbus Gemini 3-bodied Volvo B9TL 415 (BN64 CRV).

Following the transition from Edinburgh Corporation Transport to Lothian Region Transport, when the Edinburgh City Council crests were replaced with Lothian Regional Council ones, various fleetname styles were experimented with, including the large LOTHIAN side logos seen here on Alexander AL-bodied Leyland Atlantean AN68/1R 490 (MSF 490P) at Clermiston.

1984 B770 GSC was the much travelled first of two ECW Leyland Olympian 770s delivered to Lothian LRT. It was exhibited in Brussels at the UITP exhibition in May 1985. Shortly after entering service it was bought back by Leyland and refurbished for work in Thailand, before ending up with Citybus in Hong Kong. A replacement 770 arrived with the next batch as C770 SFS.

Somewhere over a rainbow – you might find Wrightbus Gemini-bodied Volvo B9TL 905 (SN08 BXV) in advertising livery for eBay. The location of the pot of gold was Sheriffhall Park & Ride.

A very popular sponsorship in recent years has been with McMillan Cancer Support. Wrightbus Gemini-bodied Volvo B9TL 856 (SN57 DFJ) wears green tartan and was named through an online poll as *Hamish*. The bus has worked on city routes and has also been loaned to Lothian Country and East Coast Buses. It was with the latter when photographed in Tranent on service 104.

Wrightbus Gemini-bodied Volvo B9TL 901 (SN08 BXP) was originally painted pale blue to promote awareness of male cancer. It then advertised the company's social media channels before settling as spare bus on Airlink service 100 before being repainted into fleet livery. The photo shows 901 crossing the border between Musselburgh and Edinburgh on service 44.

The final day of Leyland Olympians in Edinburgh was marked in 2009 by the last remaining examples running on service 15. Former coach-seated Alexander-bodied Leyland Olympian ONCL10/2RZ 369 (F369 WSC) shows the lighter red applied to a number of buses working the 15. The buses carried tram boards promoting the occasion.

Bell's Scotch Whisky was advertised on buses throughout Scotland and many companies including Lothian ran special silver and blue-liveried buses. Lothian had a few such vehicles over the years and Alexander-bodied Leyland Atlantean AN68/1R 614 (OSC 614V) represents these bright examples of advertising. It was photographed on North Bridge. (John Allison)

The painting of the silver buses was completed in Glasgow. Alexander-bodied Leyland Atlantean AN68/1R 613 (OSC 613V) was photographed at Shrubhill works prior to the blue band and side and rear adverts being applied. (John Allison)

Prior to the formation of East Coast Buses in 2016 following the withdrawal of First East Scotland from Musselburgh and North Berwick depots, Lothian Country Buses operated routes into East Lothian. Wrightbus Eclipse Urban Volvo B7RLE 173 (SN50 EDF) passes through Wallyford on service 104.

Wrightbus Eclipse Urban Volvo B7RLE 10197 (SN62 BTF) took part in the 2016 Musselburgh Honest Toun parade to promote the new East Coast Buses services that would soon be starting.

East Coast Buses launched its new fleet of 13.2-metre-long high-spec Wrightbus Eclipse Volvo B8RLEs at Archerfield House in April 2017, where 10052 (SF17 VLY) and 10054 (SF17 VMA) are seen.

A number of Lothian Buses Plaxton President Dennis Tridents were transferred to East Coast Buses mainly for school rush services, but they also appeared when needed on core services. 20625 (SN51 AYJ) heads past Wallyford Toll on the way back into Musselburgh on service 125.

East Coast Buses Wrightbus Eclipse Gemini 2-bodied Volvo B9TL 20937 (SN10 DKE) loads up at the Western General Hospital on busy service 113.

East Coast Buses Wrightbus Eclipse Volvo B8RLE 1056 (SF17 VMD) leaves Musselburgh on a Sunday working of service 140 to Roslin.

Such was the success of East Coast Buses service 124 that eight new double-deck buses were bought in 2018 to operate the service. Displaced Wrightbus Eclipse Volvo B8RLE 1055 (SF17 VMC), now working on the 106, overtakes Wrightbus Gemini 3-bodied Volvo B5TL 20008 (SJ18 NFZ) on the 124.

Wrightbus Gemini 3-bodied Volvo B5TL 20007 (SG68 LBU) is seen taking on a good number of passengers in Princes Street on an evening X24 to North Berwick.

During the summer of 2017, East Coast Buses borrowed open-top buses from Edinburgh Bus Tours to run as duplicates on the 124 service to North Berwick. Wrightbus Gemini 3-bodied Volvo B5TL 250 (SJ66 LKP), seen wearing a promotional livery for the Edinburgh Fringe, approaches Aberlady on its way back into Edinburgh.

Another open topper on hire to East Coast Buses in 2017 was Plaxton President-bodied Dennis Trident 2 217 (XIL 1480). It was photographed by the medieval fortress of Dirleton Castle.

The success of the open-top tours in 2017 prompted East Coast Buses to start up a new East Coast Tour for the summer of 2018 with its own two open-top vehicles converted from former Scania OmniCities. One of these, 20944 (SN57 DCE), was photographed at Prestongrange with a fine view of Edinburgh in the background.

A rear photo of Scania OmniCity 20944 (SN57 DCE) on the tour.

Following deregulation of bus services, Lothian Region Transport operated service 84A into Midlothian. Although normally served by buses, Duple-bodied Leyland Leopard coach 249 (NSX 249T) was photographed in Dalkeith performing the run.

East Coast Buses extended its operation into Midlothian during 2017. Wrightbus Eclipse Gemini-bodied Volvo B9TL 20794 (SN56 AEU) leaves Woodburn on its way to the Midlothian Community Hospital on service 139.

Taking a tight turning out of Aberlady on service 124 is East Coast Buses Wrightbus Eclipse Urban Volvo B7RLE 10199 (LB62 BUS). (Chris Cuthill)

Heading towards Whitecraig on service 140 is East Coast Buses Wrightbus Eclipse Urban Volvo B7RLE 10106 (RIG 6496) – formerly with Arriva and now transferred to the Lothian Country fleet.

Seen in Bathgate is Alexander-bodied Leyland Olympian 840 (J840 TSC) – now served by Lothian Country services.

1988 Alexander RH-bodied Leyland Olympian 323 (E323 MSG) is seen departing from what is now the approach to the Livingston Centre in West Lothian.

Lothian Country Wright-bodied Volvo Gemini B9TL 1046 (LKZ 5434) at Livingston Centre on X28.

Lothian Country Wright-bodied Volvo B9TL 1036 (LXZ 5422) is also on service 275 and is seen approaching St John's Hospital at Howden. (Stuart Montgomery)

Lothian Country Wright-bodied Volvo Gemini B9TL 1004 (LKZ 5386) heading through Sighthill on the X27.

Wrightbus Eclipse Urban Volvo B7RLE 10107 (RIG 6497) – formerly with Arriva and initially operating with East Coast Buses – has now been transferred to the Lothian Country fleet and was pictured at the Livingston Centre.

Repainted and being vinyled up for the MacTours open-top fleet, this is AEC Routemaster JSJ 745.

MacTours AEC Routemaster 2 (VLT 242) poses in a winter wonderland at Our Dynamic Earth. (Alistair Train)

1967 Alexander J-bodied Leyland Atlantean PDR2/1 900 (JSC 900E) was the longest lasting Atlantean in service with Edinburgh Corporation Transport. After many years in normal service it was converted to open-top. The photo shows it in its original livery and operating a diverted at Portobello part route service 15. It carried the name *The Northern Star*.

Repainted into coach livery is 1967 Alexander J-bodied Leyland Atlantean PDR2/1 900 (JSC 900E), seen on a private hire at Yellowcraigs Beach.

Lothian's second open-topper was Alexander AL-bodied 1979 Leyland Atlantean AN68A/1R 583 (JSX 583T), which had been deroofed when passing under a low bridge at Newcraighall. The bus carried a few advertising contracts during its time, including this one for BT, seen in a photo taken at Yellowcraigs Beach.

Brand new as one of a batch of five open-top buses for the Lothian fleet was 33 (W633 PSX), a Plaxton President-bodied Dennis Trident seen here passing Greyfriars Bobby. The buses would later be renumbered a couple of times and painted in City Sightseeing colours.

One of the most unusual open-toppers Edinburgh has seen: 36 (OSJ 636R) was a converted second-hand Alexander-bodied Leyland Leopard used on a special Royal Park Charabanc tour. The bus was photographed on its trip round Arthur's Seat and the Royal Park. The bus was later sold to Allens Tours of Belfast.

Fully open-top 1988 Alexander-bodied Leyland Olympian 310 (E310 MSG), named *Edinburgh Star*, circles Our Dynamic Earth.

Newly delivered City Sightseeing Wrightbus Gemini 3-bodied Volvo B5TL 229 (SJ16 CTF) is approaching the camera, while Edinburgh Tours Plaxton President Dennis Trident 511 (V511 ESC) heads the other way when the two were spotted in Holyrood Park.

A trio of open-top tour buses led by City Sightseeing-liveried Wright Gemini 3-bodied Volvo B5TL 227 (SJ16 CSZ) enters Holyrood Park.

Edinburgh Tours-liveried Wright Gemini 3-bodied Volvo B5TL 239 (SJ16 XXC) on Lothian Road.

A good load for Majestic Tours Wright Gemini 3-bodied Volvo B5TL 243 (SJ16 ZZG), which is about to leave from Waverley Bridge.

Wright Gemini 3-bodied Volvo B5TL 249 (ST66 LKO) wears a stunning wrap-round vinyl and is used on all the various open-top routes. It was displayed at the 2016 Euro Bus Expo in Birmingham.

Plaxton President-bodied Dennis Trident 512 (V512 ESC) in the livery for the short-lived Edinburgh World Heritage Official Tour. The commentary on the tour gave passengers a more detailed history of the 'City of Contrasts' than the existing ones, although most of the same tourist attractions were included.

Plaxton President-bodied Dennis Trident 651 (XIL 1484) is seen on Princes Street while commencing the Three Bridges Tour. Two Wright Volvo Geminis (905 and 906) replaced the two Tridents in 2019. (Dylan Heggie)

For a limited time during the summer of 2018, a special 20 Days of Summer Tour was operated, showing similarities to a previous Sea, City and Hills Tour run with Atlanteans some years ago. The tour took in the outskirts of the city and was not a jump-on jump-off type. Beautifully refurbished and reroofed MacTours AEC Routemasters in London Transport red and green liveries were used on the tour. Here, RM281 (VLT 281) pauses at the old Eastfield bus terminus.

Also on the 2018 20 Days of Summer Tour was AEC Routemaster RCL2241 (CUV 241C) in Green Line livery. It was photographed in Stockbridge. (Donald Stirling)

For the 2018 Vintage Bus Running Day, a surprise vehicle running a section of route 7 was AEC Routemaster RCL2241 (CUV 241C) with blinds fitted.

In June 2018, Lothian recommenced coaching after a nineteen-year gap under the banner of Lothian Motorcoaches. 9001 (SN18 CVT) is one of five Plaxton Panther-bodied Volvo B11Rs purchased and is seen shadowed by Stirling Castle on one of the many local tours offered.

By contrast, October 1984 saw the entry into service of two Duple Laser 2-bodied Leyland Tigers. 62 (B62 GSC) was pictured passing through Holyrood Park on a local tour.

1983 ECW-bodied Leyland Olympian ONTL11/2R 720 (A720 YFS) is seen in the foreground of Edinburgh Castle advertising Tennents Lager – the sponsors that year for free travel on Hogmanay.

And finally, not every bus has the fortune of being bought for preservation. Here are two Leyland Atlanteans that ended up as scrap. (John Allison)